HOOD COUNTY PUBLIC LIBRARY

AF580066

STARS OF THE
NBA

BROWN
32

THE GUARDS

BY ROBERT ARMSTRONG

CREATIVE EDUCATION / CHILDRENS PRESS

Photography

Peter S. Mecca 2, 7, 8, 11, 12, 15
Vernon J. Biever ....cover, 17, 18, 21, 22
Peter Arnold Photo Archives (Bruce Curtis) 25
Peter Arnold Photo Archives (Peter Travers) 28
Philadelphia 76'ers 26, 31
New Orleans Jazz 33, 34, 37, 39
Jerry Wachter Photography 41, 42, 45, 46

Published by Creative Educational Society, Inc.
123 South Broad Street, Mankato, Minnesota 56001

Library of Congress Cataloging in Publication Data

Armstrong, Robert, 1938-
The guards.
SUMMARY: Biographical sketches of five professional basketball guards: Walt Frazier, Nate Archibald, Doug Collins, Pete Maravich, and Dave Bing.
1. Guards (Basketball) — United States — Biography — Juvenile literature.
[1. Guards (Basketball) 2. Basketball players] I. Title.
GV884.A1A75 796.32'3'0922 [920] 76-45861
ISBN 0-87191-564-2

CONTENTS

WALT FRAZIER 6
NATE ARCHIBALD 16
DOUG COLLINS 24
PETE MARAVICH 32
DAVE BING 40

WALT FRAZIER

Rarely has an athlete or the image he presents been so well-publicized and widely accepted as has Walt Frazier of the New York Knicks.

Frazier was not Walt, but "Clyde" or "Clyde Cool." He displayed his coolness not only on the court but in his personal life.

Entering his ninth season with the Knicks in 1976, the 6-foot, 4-inch guard had built a reputation as the best defensive guard in the league. He was also considered one of its best pressure players and the equal of Oscar Robertson as a playmaker.

His style on the court contrasted with that of teammate Earl (The Pearl) Monroe, whose flashy style drew "ooohs" and "aaahs" from Knicks fans. As a pair they earned the nickname Fire (Monroe) and Ice (Frazier).

NEW YO
10

Frazier was cool because he always seemed to play within himself. There was never any wasted motion, never a change of expression on his blank face. Always being in control had its advantages, too, because after eight seasons in the NBA Frazier had not had a technical foul called on him by an official.

The desired guard combination in the NBA today features the pairing of a playmaker with a shooter.

The playmaker on most teams is responsible for bringing the ball down court and then directing the offensive patterns. He is the conductor, much like the quarterback in football.

The shooter, meanwhile, must move without the ball, seeking to get an open shot with the use of screens or rolls. These are maneuvers designed to get the shooter the ball with a clear shot or an open lane to the basket.

In Frazier the Knicks had a player who combined the best talents of both the shooter and the playmaker. While he directed the team's offense and set up teammates for open shots with his marvelous passing ability, he was also a consistent scorer. He averaged 19.5 points per game over eight seasons.

Clyde, however, was better known for his defensive play. It was a reputation he really may not have deserved. In a man-on-man situation, there were any number of players as good defensively as Frazier.

But Clyde played for the Knicks, a team dedicated to the team concept, a team in which each player protected the other on defense. Thus, if Frazier lost his man on defense, there was always someone there to pick him up and prevent an easy basket.

Because of that and Frazier's ability to steal the ball, a defensive play which captured the crowd's attention, he was named to the league's all-defensive team for seven straight years.

The Walt Frazier story began on March 29, 1945, in Atlanta. Frazier's mother still lives there with several of his seven sisters and brother.

He learned to play basketball on a dirt playground three blocks from his home and by the time he graduated from high school in 1963, he was voted the most athletic boy and the most popular boy in his class.

He played all the major sports. He was the quarterback of the football team, which he led to the city championship. He was the star guard on the basketball team and the catcher on the baseball team. At every position, of course, he was responsible for the direction of his team.

Frazier turned down scholarship offers to play football and chose a basketball grant from Southern Illinois University, a small-college power then, now a major-level school in athletics. Frazier eventually led Southern Illinois to the National Invitation Tournament championship in New York. He was named the tourney's Most Valuable Player.

It was at that tournament that he caught the eye of the Knicks and they picked him first in the college draft in 1967.

Frazier averaged only 9 points per game in his rookie season and 17.5 the next. But after that came the Knicks' glory years and Frazier was one of their biggest stars.

In a five-year period from the 1969-1970 season through the 1973-1974 season, the Knicks were the best team in basketball. They won two league championships and lost a third in the finals when their star

10

forward, Dave DeBusschere, was injured. Through that period Frazier was gaining his reputation.

"Some guys are just pressure players," Frazier has said. "I happen to be one of them. I get the feeling that I can score whenever I want to and nobody can stop me. That I can steal the ball whenever I want to."

Rick Barry, the Golden State superstar, is well aware of Frazier's abilities. "The guys I'd least like to see have the ball in the last few seconds of an important game, with the score close, are the guys who create situations," Barry has said. "To me, the best guy in this category is Walt Frazier.

"There's no way of playing him exactly right at a time like that", was Barry's comment. "You can't play him to take the jump shot, because he'll drive right around you . . . sometimes he'll get a three-point play out of it."

Under pressure Frazier has displayed his talents to their fullest. For example, in the final of the 1970 NBA title series against Los Angeles, Frazier scored 38 points and handed out 19 assists. That brought the Knicks their first title.

The statistics tell just how important Frazier was to the Knicks during their glory years. He was the leading scorer for five straight years, the assist leader for eight straight, played the most minutes for five in a row, and led the team in shooting percentage for three.

While he was performing like a superstar, he also was living like one. The $315,000 annual salary he was reportedly paid enabled him to buy closets of clothes. His seven-room, $130,000 apartment featured a mammoth round bed covered with a $3,500 mink bedspread. He drove a $20,000 Rolls Royce. He was named

America's best dressed jock by one magazine and one of the 10 sexiest athletes by another.

His main outside interest was Walt Frazier Enterprises, a company that handles athletes' contracts. The company has a staff of 12, including lawyers, controllers and secretaries, and manages the financial affairs of 40 athletes.

In addition, Frazier was able to buy his mother a home in suburban Atlanta, a $58,000, five-bedroom split-level. He pays all the family household expenses and sends both his mother and grandmother a weekly allowance.

Asked once if he had ever been criticized by other blacks for living so high, he told a reporter, "Oh, some of them say I'm not doing as much as I could to help blacks, but I say I'm an inspiration for black kids."

The Knicks went into decline following the 1974 season when three of their stars — Willis Reed, Dave Debusschere, and Jerry Lucas — retired. The team struggled into the 1975 play-offs, with Frazier averaging 21.5 points, but they were eliminated in the first round.

In 1976 there was further decline. The team did not make the play-offs, finishing last in the Atlantic Division with a 38-44 record. And, for the first time since his second season, Frazier was not among the league leaders in scoring or assists.

At the age of 30, Frazier seemed to be feeling his years. "My body is numb," he complained to reporters early in the season. "My legs are weak. I have no energy on my shots and no spring . . . Nothing seems to help. I'm worried, really worried."

With the Knicks never a threat for the play-offs, fans cheers turned to boos. Even Frazier received them. Trade rumors were heard.

But whether or not that was a sign of the beginning of the end of Frazier's status as a superstar, he had achieved what he had set out to do.

"My only goal in life was to take care of my family," he has said, "and now I've done that. When I quit playing, I'll be content to just sit back and manage all my businesses."

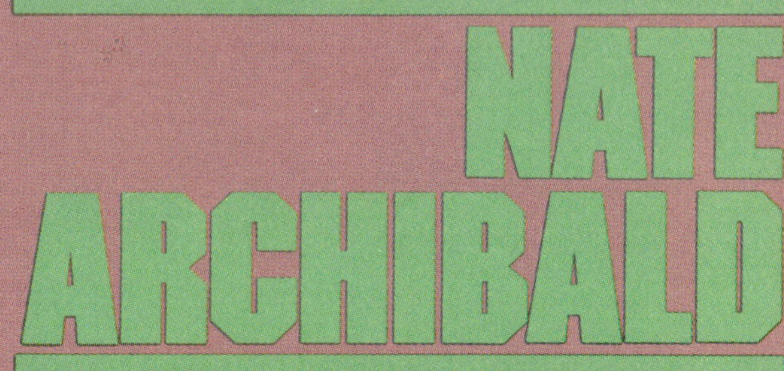

No one seems to know just how big Nate Archibald of the New York Nets really is. Last year his team's official program listed him at 6 feet, 1 inch and 150 pounds. However, there are those who say he's closer to 5-10 and that he doesn't weigh more than a sneeze.

Part of the problem is that Archibald, who prefers to be called Tiny, is constantly in motion and won't stay still long enough for anyone to get his true measurements. Anyone who has ever tried to guard him knows the problem.

Tiny was born April 18, 1948, in New York City and grew up on that city's playgrounds. He was brought up in a Bronx slum, the oldest of seven children. When Tiny was 14, his father deserted the family and Tiny suddenly found himself the man of the house. He had to help support the family and that is perhaps one of the things that saved him from the fate of many of his friends.

Kings
10
42

Between school, work and his only real interest, basketball, there wasn't much time for him to get into trouble.

But he remembers the days well.

"Some guys I used to play ball with are still standing on the same street corner they were on when I left," Tiny has said. "A lot of them are taking dope, just standing around. There's nothing you can tell them."

Much of the credit for the way Tiny turned out must go to Floyd Lane, who headed a community center in the Bronx. Lane, who later became the coach at City College of New York, is still one of Tiny's advisors.

"I couldn't make my high school team," Tiny has said. "But all I was interested in was basketball. I thought, 'Why go to school if I can't play basketball?' Floyd told me to stick in school. And he built up my confidence. I made the team in my senior year, we won the city championship, and now I'm in the big ranks."

Tiny had an ordinary career at the University of Texas, El Paso. His coach there, Don Haskins, played a controlled, low-scoring game, one that concentrated on defense. Tiny was used mainly as a playmaker. He was good, but there were other little men around the country getting the headlines.

Nevertheless, Tiny was invited to play in several all-star games after his final game as a senior. These games are mainly showcases for individual talents and are attended by all the pro scouts.

Tiny was determined to show just how good he was. He did. In one three-game tournament he scored 24, 52, and 48 points. His performance stunned his college coach and the pro scouts as well.

"I've misused this kid for three years," Haskins admitted. The Cincinnati Royals had thought they would draft Tiny because of his playmaking ability. They were thinking of offering him $25,000, not much of a salary by present-day NBA standards. The Royals suddenly found Tiny's asking price higher.

The Royals drafted Tiny on the second round and signed him to a three-year contract for $465,000. The price hurt, but former NBA superstar, Bob Cousy, then the Royals' coach, was pleased.

"I've never seen a player with his assortment of shots," Cousy said then, "and his body balance is unbelievable. Sometimes I honestly don't see how he keeps control of himself." Because that was said by a man who had more influence than any other on the way guards play the game, it was high praise, indeed.

Tiny played well his first season as a Royal, averaging 16 points per game. But he did not make the All-Rookie team. Pete Maravich and Calvin Murphy did. The next season Tiny was even better, but still he was ignored. At the halfway point of the season, he wasn't selected to play in the All-Star game.

That made Tiny angry and he decided to do something about it. He scored tremendously the latter half of the season and finished with a 28.2 average, second only to Milwaukee's Kareem Abdul-Jabbar.

Following the 1971-1972 season the Royals were sold to a group in Kansas City-Omaha. Cousy decided that the only way to draw fans to see a losing team was to have a superstar. So he changed the team's offense, concentrating on getting the ball to Tiny.

What followed was the best season a little man in the NBA has ever enjoyed. Tiny became the first player ever to lead the league in both scoring and assists, averaging 34 points and 11.4 assists per game.

But mere statistics do not tell the excitement that Tiny created. He was so good that teams used illegal zone defenses to try to stop him. They couldn't. Tiny would shoot 25-foot jump shots over them. If he was played man-to-man, no one could handle him. He would drive inside among the seven-footers and force a situation in which he was double-teamed. When that happened he would find the open man with a pass. If another player did not pick up Tiny, he would drive all the way to the basket for his own acrobatic layup.

On the fast break Tiny became one of the most feared middle men in the game because of his quickness and passing ability.

The team, too, improved, from 30-52 in 1971-1972 to 36-46 in 1972-1973.

However, Tiny was to suffer a severe test the following season. On the opening night of the season, Chicago center Tom Boerwinkle, a 7-foot, 275-pound giant,

stepped on Tiny and the little man suffered a torn Achilles tendon, one of the most feared injuries in sports.

Tiny had surgery and spent the next two months in a cast. While he was idle the team slumped and Cousy quit. When Tiny had recovered things had changed. He had gained 20 pounds, lost his speed, and his scoring average was cut in half. The team finished the season in fourth place, 26 games behind Milwaukee in the Midwest Division.

Tiny fought to get himself back in shape for the next season. And he succeeded. He averaged 26.5 points and was named to the All-Star team. With Jimmy Walker operating at the other guard position and scoring at a 19.2 average, some of the pressure was taken off Tiny. The team responded and with new coach Phil Johnson directing it, made the play-offs with a 44-38 record.

Tiny, who had been almost painfully shy in the past, changed following his injury. Floyd Lane was one of the first to notice.

"He has moved right along," Lane said then. "He isn't near as shy any more. He's changed in another way, too, in that he cares more about his body. The injury taught him that if he didn't take care of his body, he'd get fat, slow, and out of shape very easily."

The 1975-1976 season was supposed to be the year of the Kings but the team could not put it together. They were able to win only 31 of 82 games and finished third in what that season was the NBA's weakest division. Tiny, however, had another great year, and again he was named to the All-Star team.

Prior to the 1976-1977 season, Tiny was traded to the New York Nets, who were reportedly paying him $400,000 a year. The Nets were preparing for their first NBA season.

Tiny's goals remain the same on the basketball court and he has plans for when his career as a player is over.

"I'd like to do for kids what Floyd did for me," he has said. "That's why I coach two teams of kids during the summers. Kids, any kid, can approach me and ask questions because they know I'm a pro. I tell them that not everybody is going to be a pro. I tell them: Get an education, go to college, and if you have to work from nine to five, you can still have basketball."

Tiny is the proof that it is not how big a man is, but how big he plays. On and off the basketball court.

DOUG COLLINS

If you ask a child to draw a picture of a basketball player the result, as often as not, will be a stick figure, one circle for the head and another for the ball. Write the name "Doug Collins" under the picture and, presto, you have a perfect likeness of one of the NBA's next superstars!

There are so many little strange twists to the Doug Collins story that one hardly knows where to begin.

First, the Philadelphia 76ers guard is 6-foot, 6-inches tall and weighs just 180 pounds. He looks as though a strong wind might knock him over. It seems he might get killed playing against the giants in the NBA. In fact, he has the endurance of a long-distance runner, the swiftness of a sprinter. And he's as tough as a dollar steak.

Next, Collins came into the NBA as a shooter, one of the top scorers in the

20

20

country as a collegian. Now he is lucky to touch the ball 10 times a game and he has become one of the best in the NBA at playing without the ball. Still, however, he averaged more than 20 points a game in 1975-1976.

Another oddity: when the 76ers finished the 1972-1973 season, the team was a joke. It had won just 9 of 82 games. The team desperately needed a big strong center. But when the college draft came, the 76ers picked Collins.

Finally, unlike most teen-agers who grow rapidly and lose their coordination, Collins did just the reverse.

Collins was born July 28, 1951, in Christopher, Illinois. There was nothing really special about him until his sophomore year at Benton High School. Then, as a 5-8 sophomore reserve on the basketball team, he contracted mononucleosis.

When he recovered, he began to grow. Doctors cannot explain why, other than to guess that the disease somehow affected his metabolism. But he kept growing, into a 5-10 junior, then a 6-2 senior.

And as he grew, Collins' coordination developed. As a senior he made the Illinois all-state high school team and averaged 25 points. But it didn't just happen; Collins had to help it.

"It was something I really had to work on," Collins recalled later. "I did a lot of extra drills and wore a weighted vest to build up my strength. In growing, too, expecially in college when I grew four more inches, I gained quickness. I don't know how to explain it, but I never went through an awkward stage, either. And as I became taller I also became stronger."

Collins could have gone to any number of big time schools but he chose to stay close to home and attend Illinois State at Normal. Though the school has more than 18,000 students, it did not then play in a major conference.

Thus, when Collins averaged 28.6 points as a sophomore and 32.6 (third best in the country) as a junior, he remained more or less unknown. Then came the 1972 Olympics at Munich.

It was there, in the most controversial basketball game in Olympic history, that Doug Collins was almost a hero. With six seconds to play in the championship game, the United States playing Russia, Collins stole the ball. He was fouled as he drove for an easy layup. With three seconds to

JACKSON
18
20

play he stepped to the foul line. His first foul shot gave the U.S. a 49-49 tie; his second put the U.S. ahead, 50-49.

Then they played the last three seconds of the game — not once, not twice, but three times. After the third time Russia finally had a 52-51 victory and Doug Collins' heroics were lost in the controversy.

Though Collins played well enough as a senior to make All-American, he did not really gain the headlines again until the 76ers, getting first pick in the 1973 college draft, chose him. He was the first white player chosen first since Bill Bradley in 1965.

As a 76er, however, Collins got off to a slow start. He played only 25 games in his rookie season because of a series of foot injuries that required surgery and three months in a cast.

When he came back for his second season he was unsure of himself, but not for long. "I went out on the court the first time and said 'I'm gonna try to dunk,' " he recalled later. "I did and all I can remember is that I smiled."

There has been plenty of reason to smile since then.

In his second season Collins averaged 17.9 points per game, had a 48.8 field goal shooting percentage, and an 84.4 mark from the foul line. In addition, he led the team with 108 steals. At the season's end he won the Maurice Stokes award as the NBA's Comeback Player of the Year.

The 76ers' record that season was 34-48, a far cry from the 9-73 of two years before. And things were to get better.

Collins, too, was to get better. One reason was because of the change in his game. As a collegian he was expected to score a lot of points. On the 76ers he didn't have to score.

The team acquired George McGinnis, one of the best forwards in the game for the 1975-1976 season. At the other forward the team had veteran Billy Cunningham, both a shooter and a fine passer. And at the other guard was Fred Carter, a shooter who required the ball almost every time down the floor.

So Collins learned to move without the ball. To run, run, run. And run some more.

"This is something you have to want to learn," Collins explained to reporters. "It's important, too. Like how to use the screen. And it's tougher to guard a man when he doesn't have the ball. You have to move with him all the time. When you relax, you get beat."

Thus, Collins without the ball was nearly as dangerous as anyone else with it. For if Collins' defensive player relaxed for an instant, Collins would be free. If he could, he'd sneak behind a screen; if not, he'd try to find an open lane to the basket. A quick pass to Collins and the 76ers would have two more points.

Playing the game that way, and leading a devastating fast break, Collins scored 1,620 points and averaged 20.8 a game in 1975-1976. His point total was second only to McGinnis on the team and his free-throw shooting percentage of 83.6 was tops. In addition his 191 assists and 110 steals were each fourth best among the 76ers.

The team's record showed vast improvement, too. The 76ers finished with a 46-36 mark, tied for second with Buffalo. It was the first time since the 1970-1971 season that the 76ers had qualified for the play-offs.

Though Buffalo won the play-off series 2-1, Collins had three good games. He scored 13 and 20 points in the first two games. In the deciding game, however, he had his best game. McGinnis fouled out with only four field goals, but Collins scored 25 points and kept rallying the team before it finally lost in overtime, 124-123.

The most encouraging thing for the team was that it had done so well despite losing Billy Cunningham for much of the season because of injuries. Collins missed him, perhaps more than anyone, because so much of Collins' game depends on working with a good passer such as Cunningham .

The injury forced Cunningham to retire, but the 76ers added superstar Julius Erving to go along with Collins and McGinnis. The 76ers were now a definite title threat.

8 28
MOORE
12

PETE MARAVICH

Pete Maravich of the New Orleans Jazz is probably the most unappreciated player in the National Basketball Association (NBA).

"Disappointing," is what some observers say. "Never lived up to his potential," say others, or "Doesn't play defense."

All of this about a player who has a 23.9 scoring average for his six years as a pro. All of this about a player who has overcome a series of illnesses and injuries along with a little bit of personal tragedy.

Yet the criticism of Pete, though it may not be fair, is understandable. The 6-foot, 5-inch, 200-pound guard was one of the most publicized players ever to step on a college basketball court.

From 1968 through 1970 Pete was the most exciting collegian in the game. His droopy socks and flapping hair and his behind-the-back passes filled arenas across

LAKERS
JAZZ
7

7

the country. His statistics filled the record books.

Pete Maravich is the all-time leading college scorer with 3,667 points for his three-year career, a 44.2 per game average. Those figures are even more impressive when one realizes that Austin Carr of Notre Dame, the runnerup, averaged 10 points fewer for his career and totaled 1,000 fewer points.

Pete not only has the best career average, he was the two best two-year averages, 44.4 for the 1969-1970 seasons and 44.0 for the 1968-1969 seasons. He has the top three season averages, 44.5 for his final year, 44.2 in 1969 and 43.8 in his sophomore season (1968). Of the top single-game scoring leaders, Pete is the only player listed twice in the top six, with a 69-point effort in 1970 and a 66-point game in 1969.

But none of Pete's scoring abilities came as much of a surprise. Born June 22, 1948, he was groomed for the role almost from the time he could walk by his father, basketball coach Press Maravich.

"When he was a little guy asking for money for the movies," Press has said, "I'd make him earn it by pitching paper balls into a basket."

A few years later, Pete was constantly being introduced to pro players by his dad. "He just got it into his blood," Press has said, "and then one day I didn't have to bother any more — he was hooked."

After Pete became hooked, he developed the confidence he needed. One day, while still in high school in Raleigh, North Carolina, Pete was scrimmaging against such established pros as Philadelphia's Hal Greer, one of the NBA's outstanding guards. "One day," his father recalled, "Pete walked up to me after a scrimmage and said, 'You know, I think I could take Greer one-on-one.' "

By the time he was through high school, more than 100 colleges tried to recruit Pete. They never had a chance. Off he went to LSU with his dad. Freshmen then could not play on the varsity at major schools. While his father suffered a terrible 3-23 record in his first season, Pete was leading the freshmen team to a 17-1 record with a 43.6 scoring average. LSU, always a football school, responded. Fans used to crowd the arena to watch Pete in action with the frosh and then leave when the varsity game started. When Pete started putting on his show for the varsity as a sophomore, all that changed. Three years later, one of the few three-time All-Americans, Pete was ready for the pros.

The Atlanta Hawks signed him to a five-year, $2-million contract, and expected instant success. Instead they got a revolt by their veteran players, who were jealous of Pete's status as an instant millionaire. Their revolt almost destroyed the team. But with Pete making the All-Rookie team and averaging 23.2 points per game, the Hawks still qualified for the play-offs.

Then Pete's visits to the hospital began. In 1971 mononucleosis sidelined him for the entire exhibition season and the first 15 games of the regular season. He returned in a weakened condition that he battled all season.

Next it was Bell's Palsy, a disease which paralyzed Pete's face on the right side, making it impossible for him to blink his eye. In order to sleep he had to tape his eye shut.

Still he played. "I worried about someone sticking a finger in my eye and tearing the cornea," Pete told reporters. "Since I couldn't blink, the cold air rushing into my open eye hurt. I was scared worse than I had been in my whole life."

Luckily, the palsy lasted only 16 days. But to compound his problems, it was also discovered that Pete was suffering from Reiter's Syndrome, an arthritic condition in his left jaw. He was forced to exist for several weeks on milk shakes and soft foods and he lost 14 pounds.

But Atlanta was not a forgiving place. Pete had averaged 24.3 points for the Hawks. However, the team had had only one winning season in the four he was there and he was blamed. Therefore, following the 1973-1974 season, the Hawks traded Pete to New Orleans for two players and a number of draft choices.

Pete was back in Louisiana but his problems did not leave. First he suffered from severe tendonitis of the right ankle, then a hamstring pull. Then his mother committed suicide.

The physical problems had been bad enough. The latter blow was a much greater emotional shock.

Through it all, however, playing on the worst team in the league (the Jazz finished with a 23-59 record), Pete played in 79 games and averaged 21.5 points.

In 1976 things began to turn around for Pete. His defense was still a questionmark,

JAZZ
7

but he began to work his windmill offensive style into more of a team game. His scoring picked up and his passing, as always, was outstanding.

Pete has always been a superb ball-handler and few players his size have ever combined his scoring, passing, and playmaking abilities. He is one of the most feared leaders of the fast break. Once in a set offense he is doubly dangerous. He can shoot from outside or drive to the basket for a layup or force the opposition to double-team him, thus freeing a teammate for a pass and an easy two points.

The doctors still followed him around (stretched Achilles tendon and strained ankle ligament in his left leg; strained knee ligament and hamstring pull in his right) but he missed only one game in that stretch. He was elected team captain and he was optimistic. "I'm so happy down here," he told reporters, "it's the happiest I've ever been."

The new coach of the Jazz, Butch van Breda Kolff, stressed team play and movement and commented on the change in Pete.

"Our style is lots of running, which is best for Pete," van Breda Kolff told reporters. "But he's starting to slow it up when we need to. He's taking over, that's what he's doing. Right now he's playing the best I've ever seen him. If he keeps this up he's going to be a basketball player's basketball player and a coach's player, not a fan's player."

Pete missed 20 games in 1976 with injuries but he still averaged 25.9 points per game, third best in the NBA. The Jazz finished with a 38-44 record, still not in the play-offs but a big improvement over 1975. And the fans responded in huge numbers, several Superdome crowds topping the 20,000 mark and setting NBA records.

And if van Breda Kolff was right about Pete, there were better things ahead for him, and the team.

DAVE BING

Nine years after he entered the NBA things had turned topsy-turvy for Dave Bing.

When the 6-foot, 3-inch guard was drafted by Detroit in 1966, the Pistons' fans didn't want him. But when he was traded to Washington in the summer of 1975, Bullets' fans were convinced he would bring them an NBA title.

Both sets of fans were wrong and therein lies the story of Dave Bing.

When Bing reported to his first NBA training camp in 1966, he had great pressure on his shoulders. The Pistons had drafted him first, but did so only because they had lost a coin flip with the New York Knicks for the first choice in the college draft.

The Pistons had really wanted Cazzie Russell, a star at the University of Michigan. The Pistons were sure Cazzie

bullets

bullets
BROW

would draw fans into aging Cobo Arena and the Pistons needed fans as much as they needed victories.

When the $20 gold piece was flipped into the air, the Pistons' brass called out "tails." It came up "heads." The Knicks took Cazzie, the Pistons took Bing, and the next day the headline in the Detroit Free Press announced to fans: "SAD 'TAIL' — PISTONS LOSE FLIP FOR CAZZIE."

"That bothered me," Bing has said. "I knew what Detroit fans thought of Cazzie. And I thought of it constantly."

It took awhile for Bing to prove to Detroit fans that they hadn't been cheated. About half a season. An All-American at Syracuse University, he had been the team's playmaker while averaging 16 points a game. But at first he couldn't even break into the Pistons' lineup.

In his first game he took six shots and went scoreless. "It was the only time in my life I've gone scoreless," he said later. "I was really depressed. I knew I'd looked like a flop."

But that was just part of his learning process. The Pistons kept bringing him off the bench for about the first third of the season. But, gradually, he was getting more and more playing time. Finally he was playing well enough to start. Opportunity only needed to knock once for Bing.

His first start came against, of all teams, the Knicks. Bing scored 20 points. In the next game, against Los Angeles, he did everything but collect tickets at the door. Bing scored, rebounded, set up plays, played good defense, and finished with 35 points. By the end of the season, such play had become a habit, and he had a high of 47 points against Baltimore.

When his first year was over, the statistics showed that Bing had led the Pistons in scoring with a 20-point average and in assists with an average of 4.1. Those were the 10th and 11th best figures in the entire league and Bing was an easy choice as Rookie of the Year.

Detroit fans responded, too. The team, which had attracted 120,000 fans the year before, went over the 200,000 mark.

But Detroit officials felt Bing could do even more. So that summer Coach Donnis

Butcher told Bing that he was expected to shoot the ball 35 times a game. The Pistons wanted all the scoring they could get out of him.

Bing couldn't quite reach that figure the next season but he did average 25 shots a game, an increase of about 5, and boosted his average to 27.1, best in the league. In addition he was fourth in the league in assists and led the team into the play-offs.

Bing remained among the leading scorers and playmakers for the next three seasons. Then, in 1971, his career was almost ended.

Playing in a preseason exhibition game, he suffered a detached retina in his left eye. He underwent major surgery because he was told that without the operation he might lose the sight in that eye.

Four months later he was back in uniform, playing with blurred vision, but playing. Though he got into only 45 games, he still averaged 22 points.

"With a bad eye he's still better than anyone else we've got," General Manager Ed Coil told reporters.

Following his complete recovery and a full return to form the next season, Bing was awarded the Maurice Stokes trophy for his courage and determination.

But Bing became disenchanted in Detroit and asked to be traded. A year after his request, the Pistons gave in to his wishes and sent him to the Bullets in the city where he was born in November 1943.

Fans in both cities couldn't believe the trade. Only the Bullets' fans, and Bing, were happy.

The 1974-1975 Bullets had been a powerhouse, winning 60 games and going all the way to the NBA finals. But there the team collapsed and lost the championship series in four straight games to Golden State.

With Bing there appeared to be no one capable of stopping Washington. He was

bullets
21
WINTERS
32

bullets
WICKS
21
45

recognized as one of the best penetrating guards in the league and had led Detroit in scoring in five of nine seasons and in assists eight of nine. He was the third leading active scorer in the league and a three-time All-Pro.

The addition of Bing would give Washington five former members of all-rookie teams — Elvin Hayes and Wes Unseld, 1968-1969; Phil Chenier, 1971-1972; and Nick Weatherspoon, 1973-1974. Unseld had also been Rookie of the Year in his first pro season and had a Most Valuable Player award.

A team of superstars was adding yet another. "All I can bring to this team is a championship," Bing told reporters. The Bullets couldn't miss. But they did.

Bing had a fine season despite bothersome injuries. He led the team in assists with 5.9 (sixth best in the league) and averaged 16.2 points, third best on the team. But he was getting used to the Bullets and they to him. Too often, the Bullets were like a fine race car engine that had developed a miss.

The Bullets floundered, failing for the first time since the 1970-1971 season to win their division and then losing in seven games to Cleveland in the play-offs.

"I didn't expect things to be as difficult as we made them this year," Bing told reporters. "We haven't been consistent. What surprises me is how many close games we've lost. We just didn't ever seem to come up with the big play on offense or defense when we needed it in those close games. Our experience didn't show."

But though he couldn't explain the Bullets' downfall, Bing had not lost hope and was looking forward to the next season.

"We respect each other a great deal," Bing said, "and I don't care who has made a mistake . . . we have all stuck together. This is a team and no matter what happens we are sticking together and pulling for each other. I know there's no one here who is giving up or quitting."

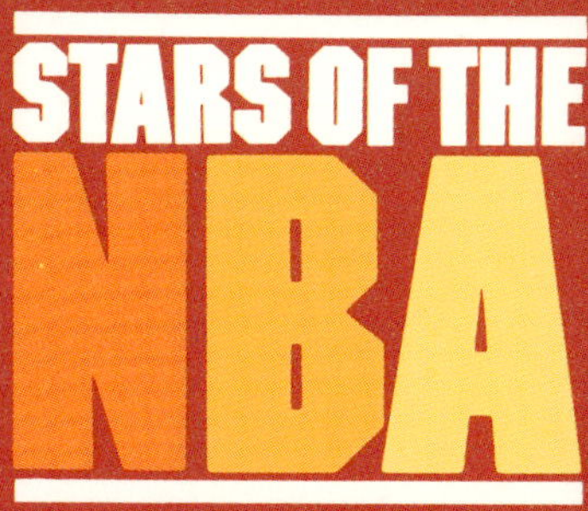

THE GUARDS
THE COACHES
THE CENTERS
THE FORWARDS